CAN YOU ESCAPE
THE NORSE
UNDERWORLD?

An Interactive
Mythological Adventure

by Gina Kammer

COMPASS POINT BOOKS
a capstone imprint

Published by Capstone Press, a Capstone imprint.
1710 Roe Crest Drive
North Mankato, Minnesota 56003
www.capstonepub.com

Library of Congress Cataloging-in-Publication Data is available
on the Library of Congress web site.
ISBN 9781666337761 (library binding)
ISBN 9781666337778 (paperback)
ISBN 9781666337785 (ebook PDF)

Summary: You are in the Underworld—the land of the dead from Norse
mythology. Ruled by the goddess Hel, it's not a place Viking warriors would choose
to go to when they die. The Underworld isn't an easy place to leave. The gods
themselves can rarely escape this cold, dark land. Can you find a way out of this
dangerous place before it's too late? It's up to YOU to choose how your story will be
told and learn the fate that awaits you in the Norse Underworld.

Editorial Credits
Editor: Aaron Sautter; Designer: Bobbie Nuytten; Media Researcher: Morgan
Walters; Production Specialist: Polly Fisher

All internet sites appearing in back matter were available and accurate when this
book was sent to press.

Printed and bound in the USA. PO4882

Table of Contents

ABOUT YOUR ADVENTURE

You are a god controlled by fate. The gods and giants are ever at odds. Trickery and betrayal hide around every corner. You don't know who you can trust. You're bound to end up in the Underworld if you take one wrong step. And who can find a way out of that cold, dark place? Can you escape your fate?

Chapter One sets the scene. Then you choose which path to take. Follow the directions at the bottom of each page. The choices you make determine what will happen next. After you finish your path, go back and read the others for more adventures.

YOU CHOOSE the path you take through this mythical adventure.

Norse myths state that the norns, three wise women named Urd, Verdandi, and Skuld, controlled the fates of the gods.

Chapter 1

A DANGEROUS FAMILY

The Norse gods are gathered near a massive root of the World Tree. It dips into the Well of Urd, a glittering spring in Asgard, home of the gods.

There, the gods are holding council as they do every day. But today is different. Odin studies the other gods as they murmur and frown. Even beautiful, bright Baldur's face is downcast.

At the well are the three norns, women who control fate. They have revealed dark prophecies about Loki's three children with the giantess Angrboda.

Turn the page.

Loki's children are the huge wolf Fenrir, the gigantic serpent Jormungand, and the powerful giantess Hel. Half of Hel's face is beautiful, with dark hair on one side. Her other half is like the dead, cold and decaying, with white hair. She will raise an army against the gods.

The norns foresee that Fenrir and the giant serpent will cause great death and destruction. The gods fear all of Loki's children.

"They're living free in Giantland," says Hermod, the nimble god. "They might betray us at any time."

Tyr, the war god, replies, "Let us bring the wolf here. Fenrir can be watched and guarded. Perhaps we can keep him chained."

The other gods look to Odin.

"Can this be done?" Hermod asks.

Odin says, "I will ask the dwarves if they can make a chain strong enough to hold him."

The gods nod their approval.

"What of the serpent?" asks Thor, the thunder god. The gods look again to Odin.

Jormungand is so large that it can circle the world and bite his own tail. Odin remains silent, thinking. Finally, he speaks. "Let me handle the serpent. I will toss him into the sea around the earth."

Thor still looks troubled, but the gods agree. Odin prepares to leave for Giantland. Tyr prepares food as bait for Fenrir, hoping the wolf will go with them.

"And what should be done with the third sibling, Hel?" Baldur asks. "She also cannot be trusted."

Turn the page.

Hel is often described with half of her face and body resembling the dead, with blackened skin and decaying flesh.

Odin pauses, looking at the rest of the gods. "I have a fitting place for her. She will have power over the worlds, but she will rule only the dead in the Underworld."

The decisions made by the gods today will have great consequences. Even the gods themselves can be tricked and betrayed as they try to gain glory or escape their destiny in the Underworld.

What role will you choose to play in the dark prophecies of the norns? Choose your path and learn what fate awaits you in the Norse Underworld.

To rule over the Underworld as Hel, turn to page 13.

To attempt a dangerous quest as Hermod, turn to page 47.

To try to escape your fate as Baldur, turn to page 73.

Chapter 2
HEL'S EXILE TO THE UNDERWORLD

Your name, Hel, means "hidden." But you don't feel very hidden as you look out over the sea. You just want to be left alone in Giantland—your home. You hear the gods coming—and they're coming for you.

First, your sibling Fenrir was somehow tricked into going with the gods back to Asgard. You know they want to control him. But Fenrir is strong. You doubt the gods can truly hold him.

Then, Odin, the All-father, used his great power to throw Jormungand into the sea.

Turn the page.

You scoff. Odin doesn't know what he's done. Jormungand is far stronger and much more dangerous than they know.

You're powerful too, but you don't know where to go. It's impossible to hide from Odin. He can use his powers to see everything from his throne in Asgard.

The footsteps of the gods grow louder as they pound over the rocky coast. You stand alone on a cliff overlooking the sea. Your huge dog, Garm, is exploring somewhere near the shore. You hope he stays safe from the whims of the gods.

The bitter winds whip through your black and white hair. But you don't feel the cold winds. With your powers, your blood runs just as cold.

You see the figures of the gods over your shoulder. Thor has his huge hammer in hand. Tyr looks ready for war, as always.

They'll be upon you in a few moments. You don't know if you should cry or laugh at how ridiculous it all is.

You look at your hands in front of you. The right is living flesh, and the other is a blackish blue—like the decayed flesh of the dead.

What can you possibly do to the powerful gods? Why do they fear you so much? You're not even sure what your powers can do. You're still learning.

Will the gods chain you up like they're trying to do to Fenrir? Or maybe they'll toss you into the sea with Jormungand. What would your father, Loki, do?

He'd probably escape with some kind of trick, you think.

Turn the page.

But you're not as clever as Loki. You don't care about such tricks.

Hide! a part of your mind screams at you in fear. *Run!* yells another. *Fight,* says a third, quietly, but determined.

You hesitate. You have only a moment to act. You don't know how to escape this fate. You don't want to be captured by the gods. But you do know one thing: you won't easily give up what's yours.

To hide from the gods in a cave, go to page 17.

To run away to the woods, turn to page 23.

To take out your dagger and fight, turn to page 28.

In a split second, you decide to hide. The gods have already seen you. But they don't know Giantland as well as you do . . . or so you hope.

You drop down into a crack in the cliff rock. Using your arms and feet, you push against the rock walls to carefully lower yourself further.

A sea cave entrance opens below the cliff face. If you can get to it quickly, the gods might not be able to find you. Maybe you can buy some time. Odin might go back to his throne in Asgard to find you, but by then, you can have a new plan.

You cling to the rocks at the bottom of the cliff. Waves crash against your body. You hold your breath and dive into the sea.

The dark opening of the cave is before you. Kicking hard, you break the surface and crawl up onto a ledge inside the cave. You wait . . . and wait.

Turn the page.

The rush of water in the cave swirls and splashes violently. You think you sense Jormungand. He must be angry.

Finally, you realize you can't wait forever. Odin has probably seen you from his throne by now. You need to move. But is it too soon?

To wait in the cave a bit longer, go to page 19.

To leave the cave and risk being discovered, turn to page 20.

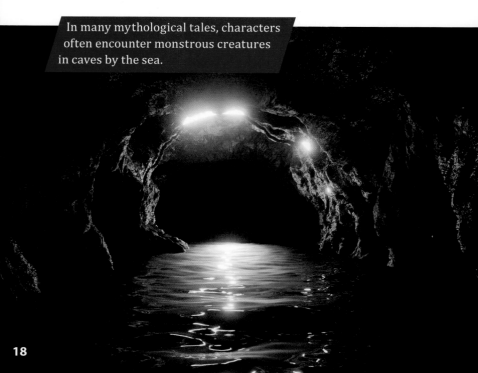

In many mythological tales, characters often encounter monstrous creatures in caves by the sea.

The water roils at the edge of your ledge. Suddenly, a great serpent tail breaks through the water's surface. But the cave is too small. The great tail crashes into the rock walls. They explode and shatter, sending shards of rock flying everywhere.

You grip the slick rock of the narrow ledge, but there's no time to escape. With a thunderous earthquake, the cave and the whole cliff above it collapse into the sea. You hope your dog is able to escape.

Your vision grows dark as you are crushed beneath the rock and sea. The prophecies about your family were right. They are very dangerous—even to each other.

THE END

To follow another path, turn to page 11.
To learn more about the Norse Underworld,
turn to page 101.

The water is roiling now. Something must be happening with the serpent. You know how massive Jormungand is. He can cause destructive earthquakes. It's not safe to stay in the cave any longer.

Quickly, you dive back into the cold sea water. You swim through the cave entrance and kick hard against the strong currents. Just as you break through the surface, you are instantly buried under another huge wave.

You swim hard and make it to a rock near the cliff and shore. You pull yourself up in time to see Thor standing at the front of a boat. He is swinging his hammer at the head of Jormungand.

The serpent swings its great head violently to the side. The motion causes another huge wave to crash over you. As soon as you can look up again, you see Thor smiling, staring right at you.

Thor, the god of thunder, and the huge serpent Jormungand are mortal enemies in Norse mythology.

Your eyes go wide in surprise. It was a trick!

Jormungand crushes the boat in his great jaws, but Thor has already jumped off. He never cared about beating Jormungand. He was after you the whole time!

Turn the page.

You cling to your rock, but Thor strides toward you across the rocky shore. Tyr and the rest of the gods follow, appearing from around the side of the cliff face.

You have nowhere to hide. Thor and Tyr pull you up from the rock. You stand, defiant, but they drag you back from the sea. Odin awaits them nearby.

"Hel, daughter of Loki," Odin greets you. "I banish you from the realm of the living."

You lick your lips, flicking your gaze to each of the gods. They surround you now. Are you ready to give up?

To try to break free from Thor and Tyr, turn to page 26.

To give up and be banished, turn to page 31.

You know you can't win if the gods catch you. In a split second, you decide to run. The gods have already seen you, but they don't know Giantland as well as you do.

You sprint away from the rock cliff by the sea and head for a wooded hillside. You hope you can lose the gods long enough to come up with a plan. Shouts rise up behind you.

As you enter the trees, you hear padded footfalls and panting. They sound closer than the gods should be.

Sneaking a look over your shoulder, you see a large mass of fur thundering after you. Its pink tongue flops in the wind. You grin. It's your dog, Garm.

Turn the page.

Your smile fades as you see the gods cresting the hill not far behind him. Garm is a good boy, and you want his help. But you don't want the gods to catch him too.

You stumble to a stop and try to get Garm to run another way. He doesn't seem to understand. He wants to play.

The gods quickly catch up to him. The god Hermod throws a stick, which sails far away from you. *Oh no*, you think. Of course, Garm goes after it.

Thor and Tyr rush to your sides and roughly grab your arms.

"Hel, daughter of Loki," Odin addresses you. "I banish you from the realm of the living."

"No!" you shout. But the other gods surround you now. They act as if they don't hear you. They've already captured you.

In Norse poems, Garm is said to be the greatest of all dogs and a guardian to the entrance of the Underworld.

GRRRR! . . . You hear a low growl behind the gods. Garm heard your cry. You're grateful that he wants to protect you. You could get him to help. But you don't want him to get hurt or captured.

To call Garm to help, turn to page 30.
To give up and go with the gods, turn to page 31.

You won't give up. This can't be your fate.

You pretend to give in and slump your shoulders in defeat. But just as Thor and Tyr loosen their grips on you, you rip yourself free. You burst through the circle of gods and run as fast as you can along the rocky shore. Jormungand still thrashes in the sea, attacking what's left of Thor's broken boat.

Jormungand was said to be so large that the serpent could circle the entire world and bite its own tail.

You start to form a plan. If you can get the serpent's attention, perhaps you can escape while he attacks the gods.

But you aren't fast enough. Hermod is the nimble god. He is swifter than anyone.

Hermod grabs your arms and you trip, falling face-first on the shore. You hit the rough rocks and your vision turns black.

THE END

To follow another path, turn to page 11.
To learn more about the Norse Underworld,
turn to page 101.

Slowly, you turn around and stand to fight. The gods stride up and spread out in front of you, trapping you against the edge of the cliff.

"Hel, daughter of Loki," Odin greets you. "I banish you from the realm of the living."

"No." You speak coldly. You won't go quietly.

The god Hermod steps toward you. You whip out a dagger and lunge toward him. But Hermod moves faster than you can believe.

He knocks your hand away, and the dagger clatters over the edge of the cliff. You scream and try to use your fists instead. Hermod dodges again.

Odin's one eye flashes with anger. "Take her," he orders the gods. Thor and Tyr, both great warrior gods, move to either side of you. They grip your arms hard.

You let the cold feeling of betrayal build in your stomach. Why can the gods seem to do whatever they want? All you wanted was to be left alone.

You know the gods have probably already won. They always get their way. But you still have one weapon left. You haven't explored your abilities much yet. However, you can feel your power growing inside you, threatening to burst out. But it's dangerous. Should you use your powers or go with the gods to your fate?

To give up the fight and face your fate, turn to page 31.

To use your powers and try to escape, turn to page 38.

"Garm!" you shout, desperate for his help. He is the largest of all dogs. You know how strong he is. He's your only chance to escape.

With a deep growl, Garm crashes into the gods surrounding you. Hermod and Baldur slam into the ground under Garm's great paws.

Tyr still holds you, but Thor lets go of your arm. Thor raises his hammer over Garm's head. Your whole world stops. Anger builds inside of you until you burst away from Tyr's grasp.

"NO!" you shout, jumping in front of Garm.

Thor's mouth opens in shock, but the swing of his heavy hammer can't be stopped. Its crushing blow kills you instantly. Garm's howl is the last thing you hear.

THE END

To follow another path, turn to page 11.
To learn more about the Norse Underworld,
turn to page 101.

You lower your head. The gods have won. Like your siblings, you can't escape your fate. You will be banished from the realm of the living. What does that mean, though? Is Odin going to kill you? You hope Garm has gotten away.

Thor and Tyr hold you tightly and march you away under close guard. Silently, you say goodbye to your homeland as you leave Midgard and Giantland. All grows cold and misty around you.

Odin calls for a halt near the deepest root of the World Tree. They have brought you to the edge of Niflheim, the world of ice and mist. You feel the power of the World Tree crackle like static. Odin seems to grow larger and more fearsome than ever.

You try to stand strong and ready for whatever happens. You already guess that they'll throw you into Niflheim, where they cannot survive. But can you? You're not sure.

Turn the page.

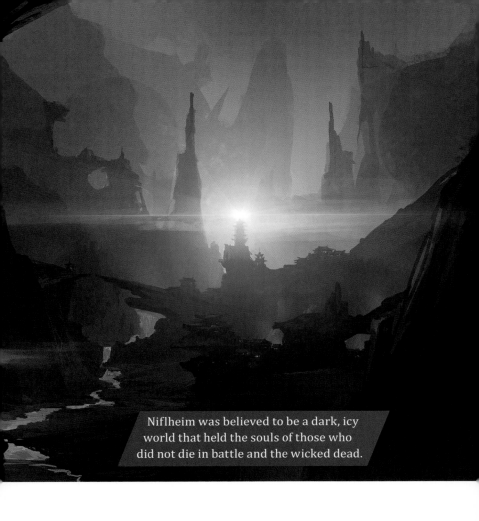

Niflheim was believed to be a dark, icy world that held the souls of those who did not die in battle and the wicked dead.

Quietly, Odin begins to chant. His breath puffs out in the cold. You feel the air buzzing with his power. His chanting grows louder and louder.

Soon a sound like roaring winds, water, and exploding ice drowns out everything else. Something great has happened in Niflheim, but you don't know what Odin has done.

"Hel, I give you authority of the nine worlds!" Odin's voice booms. "You will rule the land of the dead. It will be a place for those who do not die in glory but in sickness or from old age. You will also keep the dishonored dead."

Your eyes widen in surprise. Odin has given you a new kind of power. Yet you are as good as dead yourself in Niflheim. You open your mouth to protest, but before you can say anything, Odin gives another command.

"Throw her into Niflheim!"

Odin, Thor, Tyr, and the other gods use their great power to toss you deep into the white mists.

Turn the page.

You try to scream. But the roaring sound from before grows stronger, drowning out your cries.

You tumble down onto a sheet of ice in complete darkness. You are completely and utterly alone. The cold doesn't usually bother you, but you shiver.

Then you see a shimmer of light in the distance. Something glitters across the ice. From the other direction, you hear a mournful howl. You pick yourself up off the ice, trying to decide which direction to go.

To see what the light is, go to page 35.

To go toward the howling, turn to page 41.

The eerie howl rises again. You shudder. It almost sounds familiar, but everything is so strange in this world. No one has survived in Niflheim.

You have no idea what might be lurking here. Shaking the sound out of your head, you take a few steps toward the faint glittering light in the distance.

The darkness surrounds you like a heavy blanket. But you follow the small glint of light, trying not to stumble. Soon the sound of roaring water gets louder. You seem to walk for a long time.

Finally, you see what's reflecting a small amount of light. The roaring and bubbling is deafening as you approach the edge of a spring. It whirls like a vortex drilled into Niflheim's ice.

Turn the page.

"The Spring of Hvergelmir," you whisper. The spring is legendary, but no one has ever seen it. The World Tree's winding root plunges into the spring with a soft glow of life. Everything around it, however, is dead.

Including me, you think hopelessly.

You step around the edge of the spring to get closer to the small comfort the World Tree's root provides. But just as you're about to lay your hand on it, huge fangs snap against the root. You jump back, nearly falling into the icy spring.

"Nidhogg!" you hiss.

Nidhogg, the serpent that gnaws the roots of the World Tree, hisses back. It winds protectively around the root as it watches you. You take another step back and trip. Nidhogg's scaly head darts at you, fangs bared.

You scream and scramble backward, slipping on the icy edge of the spring. You reach out and catch a chunk of ice before you fall into the vicious whirlpool.

The serpent watches you carefully. You haul yourself back up and run into the endless darkness. The loud roaring of the spring fades behind you before you finally stop, lost and alone. You curl up against an icy hillside. You've become like the dead here, even though you're fated to live here until the end of the worlds.

THE END

To follow another path, turn to page 11.
To learn more about the Norse Underworld,
turn to page 101.

You struggle to control your unfamiliar powers. You feel the icy cold taking over. Frost quickly creeps over your skin. You see the breath of the gods as the air around you drops in temperature.

"Aagh!" cries Tyr, letting go of your frozen arm and shaking his fingers. Thor growls but holds on.

"You should be ashamed!" you yell at them, anger seething. "I'll make you regret this."

Odin begins to chant, but you know he won't be fast enough to finish his spell. Your power won't stay contained any longer. It explodes from you in shards of ice and force.

You see the gods blown back by your power. Odin shouts into the gale. Thor's grip on you loosens, and he is sent tumbling over the cliff. Baldur stares up at you from the ground, cold and lifeless.

In Norse mythology, Hel has power over the dead, but the tales don't give details about what types of powers she has.

Turn the page.

But you don't know how to stop. The power
keeps exploding from you. It's too much. You can
feel yourself being torn apart. Soon you give in
to the power as it takes your life. Odin has won
after all.

THE END

To follow another path, turn to page 11.
To learn more about the Norse Underworld,
turn to page 101.

The eerie howl rises again, causing you to shudder. But suddenly, you stop. You know that howl! Did the gods banish Garm too? Or did he somehow follow you on his own?

"Garm?" you call into the darkness, taking a few steps in the direction of the howl. You see nothing but a faint reflection off the ice.

The howl sounds again, and this time you're sure it's familiar.

"Garm!" you shout louder, desperately.

Like the good boy he is, the dog's massive form bounds up to you, tongue drooping from his mouth. You throw your arms around the furry beast as he licks you and dribbles drool everywhere. But you don't care. You're too happy to see him.

"How did you get here? I thought the gods would kill you!" you tell him in wonder.

Turn the page.

In response, Garm sits and pants, looking up at you with pure doggy love.

"Well," you say, "it looks as if the cold doesn't bother you either. Good."

You scratch his ears as you think. Having Garm next to you makes your fate feel much less awful.

"Hmm . . ." you think aloud. "What do you say we try out my powers? See what they can do."

Garm barks excitedly. Then he bounds off, looking back at you expectantly. You follow him over a bridge to a break in the ice.

A yawning opening, like a cavern entrance, stands before you. You gasp, realizing that this must be what Odin had been doing with his magic. He was creating a new sort of world—the Underworld. The land of the dead.

You then remember what Odin said. He gave you authority over the nine realms. And he instructed you to keep a place for the dead from those worlds.

You turn and give Garm a smirk. "Odin wants me to rule? Well then, I should have a palace, shouldn't I?"

Garm starts barking and wagging his tail, running in circles around you.

Stepping through the opening, you call upon your power. You feel the ice in your very core. Here, using your powers feels natural and easy. You wonder if that was another effect Odin's magic had on you and this place. Here, you feel you have purpose.

You focus your attention on the center of the cavernlike space in Niflheim. You stretch out your hands, and the ground begins to rumble.

Turn the page.

Then you raise your hands, and a great palace forms. It rises from the ground, stretching up until you can stretch your hands no farther. Icy and golden, your palace gleams before you. You're surprised at your own abilities.

You grin and run toward the palace with Garm. "Next, we'll build mansions for the dead— great and tall! And we'll put up a wall with strong, high gates. Odin wants me to have authority. Very well. I'm going to make the most of it!

"And if I can't leave," you continue, "neither will anyone else. No one who comes through that gate will leave again. I won't give up what's mine."

You feel the truth of your words. Extending your power, you feel the lives of everyone in the nine realms. And you can feel it the instant one of those lives ends.

Hel's great palace was named *Eljudnir* in Old Norse. In English the name means "sprayed with snowstorms" or "damp with sleet or rain."

"Come," you tell Garm. "We need to get ready for our guests. They'll be here soon."

You enter your huge palace and step into the throne room. You walk up to the throne and take your seat. It is time for you to rule the Underworld.

THE END

To follow another path, turn to page 11.
To learn more about the Norse Underworld,
turn to page 101.

To protect her beloved son, Baldur, Frigg made all living creatures promise that they would never harm him.

Chapter 3

HERMOD'S MISSION

Your friend Baldur is dead—gone to Hel in the Underworld, where you and the other gods threw her. Odin gave Hel power to rule the dead, and now she rules over Baldur too.

You stare in shock as you look down at the once bright and cheery Baldur. In death, his light has gone out. You think you should be crying—wailing as hopelessly as Baldur's mother, Frigg.

Frigg foresaw Baldur's death. So she had made everything in the universe give an oath to never harm Baldur. Everything except poisonous mistletoe. The plant was so small and young, she didn't think it was a threat.

Turn the page.

You glare at Hod, Baldur's blind brother. Hod threw a spear made from mistletoe that killed Baldur. Hod just looks confused.

You clamp your teeth together hard. You wish you could do something. But you're not as famous as Thor or Tyr. You're just Hermod. Hermod the nimble.

Frigg's voice rings out. "Which of you will gain glory and go to Hel? If you make her release Baldur back to us, you'll earn my favor."

You and the other gods stare at her, silent. The road to the Underworld is dangerous. If you enter Hel's realm, you may get stuck in the Underworld forever. But perhaps this mission could make you Hermod the brave.

Frigg is desperate. "Find Baldur. We will give Hel a ransom in return. Bring him back to Asgard."

Frigg offered honor and glory to any of the gods who would go to Hel and bring Baldur back to her.

You wonder if a ransom might work. You open your lips to speak. But should you volunteer? Surely Thor or Tyr would be better for the job. Yet no one speaks.

To volunteer to rescue Baldur, turn to page 50.

To vote for someone else to rescue Baldur, turn to page 56.

"I'll go," you say, surprising yourself. "I'll bring Baldur back!" Your voice sounds much more certain than you feel.

Frigg nods to you in respect.

You feel a little sick and proud at the same time. You're really doing it. You're going to meet Hel, ruler of the Underworld.

"Fetch Sleipnir!" Odin orders. The eight-legged stallion soon gallops up to you.

"Hermod," Odin says, turning to face you. "You are the swiftest rider we have. Take my steed, and ride fast!"

You gulp but nod and take the reins. You climb onto the back of the majestic beast and say goodbye. Then you head into the darkness of the road to Hel and the dead.

You ride for nine nights. The days look no different, and you can see nothing. But Sleipnir seems to know the way. The air grows colder as the road leads ever downward.

You hear a deep growl as you approach an even deeper darkness like a yawning cave. You know the entrance to the Underworld is guarded by Garm, the vicious hellhound.

Urging Sleipnir to go faster, you close your eyes as he makes a great leap through the cave entrance. A howl sounds behind you. You shiver as you realize you must have leaped past the hellhound.

But the beast let you pass unharmed. You wonder if he guards the Underworld from those coming in—or those trying to leave.

Through the darkness and mist, you see something shine with a soft, golden light.

Turn the page.

"Over there," you tell Sleipnir, although the horse seems to know where to go.

You ride up to a bridge covered in gold. A flood of icy waters rushes beneath it. You can see weapons flowing by in the water. Swords and axes clang against each other in the fierce currents.

Sleipnir steps cautiously over the golden bridge. You're so busy watching the spears and shields tear through the water that you don't notice the giantess blocking your path.

"I am Modgud, the furious battler," she says. "What is your name? Who are you? Your steps over the bridge are louder than the five battalions of the dead that just crossed. You do not look as pale as they were. Why do you travel on the road to Hel?"

The giantess Modgud stood guard at the bridge over the river Gjöll. She did not allow the dead to return to the land of the living.

The guardian of the bridge looks fearsome. You wonder if she'll let you pass if she knows you're not one of the dead. You hesitate before giving Modgud your answer.

To tell Modgud the truth, turn to page 54.

To lie to Modgud and say you're dead, turn to page 60.

Modgud steps closer. You realize that lying is useless. She already knows you're not dead.

"I am Hermod," you answer. "I have come to seek Baldur. Has he come here?"

"Yes. The beautiful Baldur rode over this very bridge," she says.

"Do you know where he is?" you ask.

"He has gone to the hall of Hel. Ride down and north. That is where you will find him."

"Thank you!" you say, and ride on as Modgud allows you to pass. You're surprised how easy it was to get by her. Perhaps too easy. . .

The roaring of the Gjöll River fades behind you. Eventually, you come up to high walls and Hel's gate, called the Corpse Gate. You shiver. Through the gate is the realm of Hel where the living do not go. You pause before the high gate.

"What should we do, Sleipnir?" you ask, patting the stallion's neck. "Do we dare go through the gate?"

Sleipnir stomps his eight hooves and snorts. He doesn't like the idea of going through the gate either. You look around, wondering if there's another way. But the walls are even higher than the gate.

To go through the gate, turn to page 58.

To find another way, turn to page 62.

A growl rumbles in the back of Thor's throat. He's scary when he's angry. But still, no one accepts Frigg's mission.

You close your mouth, hesitating. Were you really about to volunteer to take the road to Hel? You're not as mighty as Thor or as great a warrior as Tyr or the others.

"It should be Thor," you say suddenly, surprising yourself for speaking up at all.

Thor shoots a dangerous glare at you. You shrink back, but the other gods quickly voice their agreement.

"Yes," says Tyr. "Thor will have the best chance of making it out."

Frigg nods, and Thor sighs.

"I will go," Thor finally agrees.

"Go quickly," says Odin. "I give you my steed, Sleipnir, to ride. May he bear you well."

The stallion with eight legs trots up to Thor. Thor mounts and begins to ride.

"You will have my love and glory forever!" Frigg promises Thor, shouting after him.

Your heart sinks. Thor is large and heavy. Even Sleipnir can't carry him as quickly as he needs. Somehow, you already know that Thor's mission is doomed. He wasn't the right god to send to Hel. But you didn't speak up when you should have. Now it's too late. Your hopes of gaining glory or of ever seeing Baldur again fade away.

THE END

To follow another path, turn to page 11.
To learn more about the Norse Underworld,
turn to page 101.

You take a deep breath and urge Sleipnir up to the gate. Soundlessly, the great doors swing inward. Through the gate, you see Hel's great hall rising in the distance.

"Go on," you tell Sleipnir. He shakes his mane but obeys.

Immediately, the Corpse Gate clangs shut and locks behind you. You turn quickly, but you see that there's no way to open the gate again. You breathe hard. It already feels like you can't get any air—as if you are dead.

"Let's go find Hel," you say in a low voice.

At Hel's palace, you find Hel and Baldur seated in her hall. Baldur is eating with his dead wife, Nanna, at Hel's table. Hel sits on her throne, watching you with a dark expression.

"Hermod!" Baldur greets you. "My friend. So you've come to keep me company!"

"Well, no," you say, swallowing hard. "I'm here to bring you back to Asgard with me."

Baldur glances at Hel. "Hermod," he says, "you entered through Hel's gate. You cannot leave again."

You feel ill. Bringing your hand to your face, you place it on your cold skin. "No," you say in barely a whisper. "This can't be. I was sent by Odin himself."

Hel, half living and half dead, rises from her throne and steps down to you, moving gracefully. "Baldur is right, Hermod," she says with a wry smile. "I keep what is mine."

You realize your mission is lost, and you are doomed to stay here until the end of the worlds.

THE END

To follow another path, turn to page 11.
To learn more about the Norse Underworld,
turn to page 101.

"Well? Why are you entering the land of the dead?" Modgud prompts you.

You quickly decide that it's better to lie about who you are. Modgud probably won't let you cross into the land of the dead while you're alive. But it's very dark. You hope she won't be able to tell that you still live.

"My death was quick," you answer. "I couldn't bear it after my friend, Baldur, was killed. It stopped my heart, and here I am to join him." You hope the lie will help you learn where Baldur is.

Modgud narrows her eyes and steps closer. You nudge Sleipnir to take a couple of steps back on the bridge. You don't want Modgud to get too close. She might see you're not actually dead. Modgud follows you back to the middle of the bridge.

"You're not dead!" she says accusingly.

"Yes, I am," you say weakly.

Modgud gives you an evil smile. "No, you're alive. But not for long."

Using her great spear, she strikes you off Sleipnir's back and into the icy river. The weapons of the dead hit you from all sides, and the river washes you into complete darkness.

THE END
To follow another path, turn to page 11.
To learn more about the Norse Underworld, turn to page 101.

You jump off Sleipnir's back. "I don't like the look of those gates," you tell him. "I can tell you don't either. I don't think we'll be allowed to go home if we go through them."

Sleipnir whinnies.

"Do you think you can jump over them? Maybe we can sneak in that way."

Sleipnir whinnies again and stomps eagerly.

You tighten his saddle and get back on. You ride back a distance from the gate. Then you spur Sleipnir on.

"RUN!" you shout.

Sleipnir gallops faster than ever before. At the last moment, Sleipnir springs off the ground from his four back legs and nearly flies. He clears the gate and lands at a run on the other side—in the realm of Hel.

Turn the page.

Odin's horse, Sleipnir, was called the greatest and fastest of all horses. He is usually described as having eight legs. Sometimes he is said to have wings to be able to travel to places where even the gods cannot go.

You slow as you bring Sleipnir up to Hel's palace. You leave him outside as you enter her great hall. Immediately, you see Baldur sitting at the head of the table. Nanna, Baldur's wife, sits at his side.

You smile, happy to see your friend again. Baldur smiles back, although he looks pale and no longer shines with his usual bright beauty. You go to him and sit at his other side.

Hel sits across the hall in her throne. You know it's her instantly. Her dark hair flows down her right side while her left side is covered by white hair. It partially covers the corpse-colored skin of the left side of her face.

"I've come to ask that you let Baldur return with me to the lands of the living," you call to her, rising from the table.

"I rule the dead," Hel says simply. "I do not give up what is mine. Why would I let Baldur go?"

You think carefully about how you should answer. Frigg said you would have to offer Hel a ransom. Everyone weeps for Baldur, and he is missed among the gods. Surely Hel won't ignore all who mourn, would she? What would persuade Hel to give Baldur up?

To offer Frigg's ransom,
turn to page 66.

To plead that all mourn for Baldur,
turn to page 68.

You decide to follow Frigg's advice. "Frigg sent me to bring this message . . . she will give you a great reward for returning her son to her," you say and wait.

"A ransom?" Hel laughs coldly. "What could she possibly give me? Baldur is a prize like no other. Never has such beauty entered my halls. I would be foolish to give him up."

You open your mouth and then close it, not knowing what else to say. "Name your price. Let me take it back to Frigg. I'm sure she will pay any cost."

"Tell her this," Hel says. "The gods should have thought about their actions before sending me here to rule. Baldur has come to me as one of the dead. He is treated with honor here and drinks my mead and eats my food. He sits with his wife. He belongs here—with me."

You pale at her commanding words. You didn't expect to fail. But was the failure yours or the gods'? After all, you are only their messenger.

"Go!" Hel orders you. "I will let you leave through the gate, but you shall never return—until it's your time to stay here with me."

Hel gives you a wicked smile before you turn and rush out of her hall.

THE END

To follow another path, turn to page 11.
To learn more about the Norse Underworld,
turn to page 101.

You doubt there's any ransom that will make Hel give up Baldur. Instead, you hope Hel still has some compassion.

"Please," you beg, "let Baldur ride home with me. All of the gods, all of creation, weeps for Baldur. The world is darker without him. Everyone loves him and mourns his loss. Will you not return him to us?"

Hel raises a dark eyebrow. "What should I care? The matters of men and gods do not concern me."

You try harder, falling to your knees. "Please! Everything weeps for Baldur. Not just gods and men! But every animal. Every giant. Even the trees, the stones, and oceans! Let him come back with me."

Hel doesn't say anything at first. Then, quietly, she asks, "Even the dead?"

Turn the page.

When Hermod the nimble finally found Baldur in Hel's hall, he begged Hel to allow his friend to return to Asgard.

You nod. "Even the dead mourn for Baldur. There are none that do not love him."

"Prove it," she says dangerously. "If all things in the world, alive and dead, weep for him, then I will know that he is loved as well as you say. I will let him go back to you. But if there is even one that does not mourn, then I will keep him forever."

You scramble to your feet. "Yes! Yes!" you say. "I will send out every messenger to ask everything if it grieves for Baldur. You will see!"

Hel looks skeptical, but she motions for Baldur to speak to you. Baldur offers you Odin's ring, which was placed on his funeral pyre. "Take this back to Odin, so he knows you were here." Then Nanna gives you other gifts to take back for Frigg.

"Go," Hel says. "The gates are opened for you."

With a huge grin, you ride out of Hel and return to Asgard. Finally, you see the light of day again. Eagerly, you ride to Odin's hall to give the gods the news that not all hope of rescuing Baldur is lost.

* * *

You've succeeded in your mission to find Baldur. But in the end, your efforts to bring him home fail. The gods send out many messengers to see if everything weeps for Baldur. But Loki plays another of his cunning tricks. Disguised as a giantess, he refuses to weep.

"Baldur never did me any good," Loki says. "Let Hel keep what is hers."

So she does. Hel never allows Baldur to leave.

THE END

To follow another path, turn to page 11.
To learn more about the Norse Underworld,
turn to page 101.

Odin's son Baldur often had nightmares that foretold his own death.

Chapter 4
Baldur's Fate

You gasp as you wake from yet another nightmare. You dreamed that you were pierced with an arrow and are bleeding. Hel was pointing at you with a glare. She was angry that you and the other gods threw her into Niflheim. But Odin gave her power to rule over the dead there, and she was claiming you for herself.

Feeling your chest, you're happy to find no arrows or wounds. You wipe sweat from your forehead. It was just a nightmare.

"Baldur!" your mother calls you. "Get up! I have wonderful news."

The goddess Frigg, your mother, enters your chambers as you groggily get out of bed.

Turn the page.

"Your father has given me advice about your nightmares. He believes they're true dreams of the future."

You stare at her with wide eyes. "And this is good news?" you splutter.

"Well, no," she admits. "But I've made sure that nothing can harm you. Everything in the cosmos has taken an oath not to harm you. Now your dreams can't come true!"

You give your mother a shaky smile. "Umm, thank you?"

Frigg sighs. "You don't believe me."

"I don't know what to believe right now!" you say, baffled.

"Come, I'll show you." Your mother leads you out to a gathering of the Aesir gods. They stand in a circle, and Frigg pulls you into the center.

"Go on!" she tells them.

The gods raise various weapons, stones, and cages of angry animals. They all stare at you.

"What are you doing?" you cry out, seeing where this is going.

Your nightmare comes back to you in a dark flash. This is all too familiar. You see the gods coming at you, and your instinct is to run. But your mother smiles at you encouragingly. Do you stay?

To trust Frigg's promise that you won't be harmed, turn to page 76.

To run and avoid the risk of getting hurt, turn to page 79.

You realize you can't run from your own mother. Yet you're terrified of what's about to happen. The gods obey Frigg when she urges them to strike. Thor swings his hammer. Tyr heaves a heavy stone. Frigg herself opens a basket and flings a venomous snake at you.

You cower, shutting your eyes tight and covering your face. Thor's hammer falls. The rock flies. The snake bites.

But suddenly, everything stops. You open one eye, then the other. Not one blow, strike, or bite landed on you. You feel your chest, your arms, and your legs. Everything is fine.

"Woohoo!" You cheer and grab your mother in a bear hug. "You did it! You really did it!"

"Of course, I did," she says, sounding offended. But a smile spreads across her face.

The gods took turns testing
Baldur's invincibility to see
if Frigg's promise was true.

Turn the page.

Then the gods make it a game. They try to strike you with everything they can think of. But nothing touches you. You feel invincible!

Then Loki brings over Hod, your blind brother. He wants to join in the fun too. He's hefting a sharp spear and getting ready to hurl it at you.

To keep testing your invincibility,
turn to page 81.

To call for a stop to the test,
turn to page 90.

You love your family, but you don't trust them enough to let them attack you. You run between Thor and your mother.

"Sorry!" you shout over your shoulder. "I don't think this is a good idea!"

"Baldur!" Frigg calls. "They can't hurt you!"

"That's great!" you shout, but you keep running.

Maybe your mother is right, and they can't hurt you. But you don't need to tempt fate. You have plenty of time to test her promise later. You'll return to the gathering when the other gods aren't so eager to throw their weapons at you.

Your dream of Hel still haunts you. Somehow, you don't think she'd let you go if you ever entered her realm. You'd rather spend more time with your wife and son first.

Turn the page.

"Nanna!" you call to your wife as she walks through the gardens of Asgard. "May I join you?"

Nanna looks up and smiles. "Of course, my love."

You take her hand and enjoy every moment of being alive.

THE END

To follow another path, turn to page 11.
To learn more about the Norse Underworld, turn to page 101.

Tyr swings his ax at you, determined to land a blow. But it just slices through the air without touching you. You laugh. Tyr laughs too. You feel indestructible.

But at that moment, a wooden spear flies into your chest. But it doesn't stop and fall like the other weapons. Just like your dream, it pierces you all the way through.

Your smile falters. Stumbling back, you look up and meet Hod's sightless eyes. A hush has fallen over the gathering of gods.

"What happened?" says Hod. "Someone, tell me what happened!" He seems panicked. Behind him, Loki grins at you wickedly.

"Poisoned mistletoe!" You hear your mother hiss. Then she wails as she catches your bleeding body. "NO! No! I didn't think I would need an oath from such a small plant!"

Turn the page.

You feel your strength fading. Your view of the gods around you blurs. Soon, your lifeless body slumps to the ground.

You are dead.

* * *

You wake to find a world of darkness around you. Cold mist closes in on you. You feel as if you're moving downward, but you see nothing.

Hod! You try to growl, but you seem to be formless, without a voice.

You should be celebrating with the gods! You're not supposed to be . . . wherever you are. You want to get revenge on Hod. How had he hurt you when none of the others could? He must have known the one thing your mother didn't get an oath from. He wanted to kill you. You seethe with anger.

Aahhwwooooooooo! A chilling howl pierces the nothingness.

Then you see a soft, warm glow. Suddenly, you're standing before a golden bridge. But under the bridge rushes icy water filled with clashing blades and weapons. You shiver. You must be in the Underworld.

Turn the page.

Only the dead could easily travel to the Underworld. The living needed special magical abilities to travel there and survive.

The bridge seems to offer the only light. Yet you're pretty sure that if you cross it, there will be no way back. When you look behind you, you see only darkness and mist. But you think you see the faint outline of an opening, like a cave entrance, through the mist. Which way should you go?

To run to the cave entrance,
go to page 85.

To cross the bridge,
turn to page 87.

A spray of icy water hits your face, and you quickly step back. You didn't realize you'd gotten so close to the river. But now you see the weapons for what they are—the weapons of the dead. On the far shores, you think you see the pale forms of the dead fighting in some pointless battle.

No. You are a god. You can't die. *This can't be happening,* you think. You don't belong here!

You turn and run. The faint outline of an arch rises ahead of you. Your feet pound the road leading upward, yet they hardly make a sound.

It's just the mist, you think. And the darkness. Everything is muffled.

A low growl rumbles as you approach the opening. You search the darkness for the source of the sound, but it's impossible to see anything.

Turn the page.

You look back toward the cave entrance only to see two gleaming eyes. You skid to a stop, but you're too close. The creature leaps, and two huge, dark paws slam into your chest.

The hellhound! you realize too late. The guardian of the Underworld knocks you into endless darkness.

THE END

To follow another path, turn to page 11.
To learn more about the Norse Underworld,
turn to page 101.

The light of the bridge tempts you. It's the only thing that looks inviting in this dark place. You decide to cross and see what's on the other side.

Your steps barely make a sound as the river roars under you. When you look up again, you're startled to see a woman in armor waiting for you.

"I am Modgud," she tells you. "I guard the Gjöll Bridge. Who are you, and why do you enter Hel's realm?"

"I am Baldur," you answer. "But I am not meant to be here. My brother—"

Modgud interrupts you. "Oh, yes, you are. Baldur, son of Odin, we've been waiting for you."

You shut your open mouth, confused why anyone would be waiting for you here. But as you're about to argue with her, Modgud speaks again.

Turn the page.

"You may pass. Go down and northward. There you will find Hel's high hall. Her mead is being prepared for you."

You step off the bridge, feeling Modgud's eyes watching you. You decide to follow her direction—at least for now.

But once she's out of sight and you're farther down the road, you pause. You see another castle in the distance, off the main road. You wonder if it might reveal another way out of this place . . .

To continue to Hel's hall, turn to page 92.

To go to the other castle, turn to page 97.

Along with Hel's great palace, another dark castle called Nastrond faced toward the north.

You decide you have all the proof you need that Frigg's plan worked.

Just as Hod hurls his spear, you duck and cry out, "Enough!" The spear flies harmlessly over you.

"I must tell my wife and boy the good news!" you say.

You laugh, clapping Tyr on the shoulder with one hand. "Let us celebrate. I've been so worried by my dark dreams. This is just what I needed to put the worries behind me!"

Tyr and Hod congratulate you on your success. Loki scowls, but you never know what the trickster god is thinking. He's probably mad that you ended the game.

Frigg's eyes meet yours, and you give her a nod and smile. She's the reason you no longer have anything to fear.

You feel so relieved to know nothing can hurt you. You spot Nanna, your wife, and run to her.

"Nanna! You'll never guess what's happened . . ."

THE END

To follow another path, turn to page 11.
To learn more about the Norse Underworld, turn to page 101.

You continue on the road, despite how much it feels like your nightmare. You're sure Hel is still angry with you and the other gods for throwing her into Niflheim.

Dreading what awaits you, you approach the tallest gate you've ever seen. You shudder as it silently swings open for you.

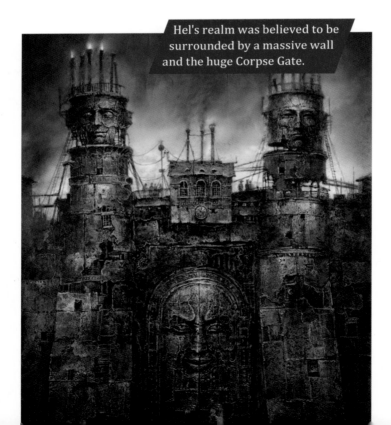

Hel's realm was believed to be surrounded by a massive wall and the huge Corpse Gate.

Slowly, you step through. Inside the walls of Hel's realm, everything changes. It still looks like the Underworld, but there are rich mansions everywhere.

In the center, Hel's palace rises before you. You are awed by its golden walls and decorations. The dead go about their business, doing all the things they would normally do in life.

Gathering your courage, you enter Hel's hall. A woman with dark hair flowing down one side and white hair down the other greets you.

"Hel," you say, surprised.

Hel gives you a crooked smile. "Baldur, welcome. A place has been prepared for you."

She shows you to a seat at the head of the table. You sit down in a daze. Servants place food before you. A woman pours a goblet of mead. The Underworld isn't what you expected.

Turn the page.

You take a sip of the mead and a few bites of food. All of it is good, but it doesn't seem quite right, either. Then you remember that you are dead, and Hod, your betrayer, still lives. He still enjoys the feasts and parties of the living while you are stuck here.

"No," you say, pushing away from the table. "I need to go back to Asgard. My life . . . ." you trail off.

"Is ended," Hel finishes for you. "You belong to me now. But do I not treat you well? Look, I have a surprise for you."

Hel points to the door of her hall. A woman is led inside. As she enters the light, you see it is your wife.

"Nanna!" you cry and run to her.

She hugs you tightly. "Baldur, I couldn't bear it. My heart gave out from grief."

You feel so torn. You're happy to be with your wife. But she has died out of grief for you. She should still be enjoying life. It's all Hod's fault. Your anger rises again.

"Her seat is now next to yours," Hel says. She leads you both back to sit at the table.

Later, Hermod, the swift god, enters the hall. You hardly look up at him. You feel so defeated. But Hermod makes a deal with Hel to let you go. Hope sparks in you again. You give Hermod a ring and gifts to take to Odin and Frigg. He leaves to give them the news so they can confirm that everything on earth weeps for you. If everything does, Hel will let you go.

You wait.

Then one day, Hel summons you to her throne. She looks smug as you stand before her with Nanna by your side.

Turn the page.

"I give you news from the gods," she says.

"Did everything weep for me?" you ask, daring to hope.

"Absolutely every god, rock, tree, ocean— everything," she begins. You start to smile, hardly believing it.

"However," Hel continues, "one old giantess did not weep. So you are mine. I will never give you up." Her lips curl into a wicked grin.

Your smile fades, but then you look at Nanna. At least you're stuck in the Underworld with your true love.

THE END

To follow another path, turn to page 11.
To learn more about the Norse Underworld, turn to page 101.

Your dream haunts you as you look down the road toward Hel's castle. You know Hel won't give you up once she has you. But she doesn't have you yet—not completely.

You step off the main road and head left, walking through the wasteland toward the other castle. Finally, you approach the gates. They're shut tight, so you use the crumbling grooves in the wall to climb over. There's no one around.

When you drop to the ground inside the wall, you hear shrieks and a hiss coming from the large hall. Cautiously, you enter. But you are immediately trapped.

The floor itself writhes as snakes coil up your legs. You scream and kick them off, but more take their place. Snakes are everywhere. They slither up the walls.

Turn the page.

Further inside, you see the dead. Most of them no longer fight the snakes. Some cry out as something drips from the vent in the ceiling. The wet dripping sizzles as it hits the dead, burning them like poison acid.

You try to back out of the door. You realize now what this place is. It is Nastrond, the place where evildoers are punished. There is no escape.

"I was wrong," you say to yourself, backing toward the door. But just as you make it out, the serpent Nidhogg strikes. The great snake's fangs clamp down on your shoulder, and it drains your blood. You scream as you are shoved back into the hall of poison and serpents.

THE END

To follow another path, turn to page 11.
To learn more about the Norse Underworld,
turn to page 101.

In Nastrond, the wicked dead were believed to be tormented by poisonous snakes and the terrifying serpent Nidhogg.

Loki had several children with Angrboda (left).
They included Jormungand the giant serpent,

Chapter 5
THE UNDERWORLD

We don't know much about the Norse Underworld or its ruler from the mythology. We do know a little about their origins as reported in the surviving tales.

They state that Loki had three children with the giantess Angrboda. Their children were feared by the gods. Prophecies said that Loki's children would bring destruction. So the gods decided to capture or contain them to try to change their fate.

One of Loki's children, Hel, was banished to the Underworld to keep her from becoming a threat. However, Odin still gave Hel some power to provide a place for those who died from illness or old age.

The Underworld's entrance was guarded by Garm, the large hound of Hel. The giantess Modgud stood guard upon a golden bridge spanning a river full of weapons. Inside high walls through the Corpse Gate, Hel kept the dead who did not die in battle.

The dead lived in mansions and ate, drank, or fought in battles just as they did while alive. Yet everyone was pale, they couldn't travel to the other worlds, and their ruler was harsh.

In one example of Hel's power and rule, she claimed the beautiful god Baldur as her own. When Baldur's mother, Frigg, learned that her beloved son would die, she tried to change his fate. She went throughout the universe and made everything promise not to harm Baldur. However, she neglected to get a promise from the small mistletoe plant.

Loki, the trickster god, had never liked Baldur. He was jealous because Baldur was loved so much by all the gods.

Loki disguised himself as an old woman and went to talk with Frigg. He asked her if everything had truly sworn to never harm Baldur. She admitted that she had not made the mistletoe plant swear an oath. She thought it was so small that it couldn't harm her son.

After Loki learned about the mistletoe, he made a poisoned spear from it. Later, as the gods tested if Baldur was truly indestructible, Loki decided it was time to use the spear.

Hod, the blind god, felt left out of the gods' game. Loki gave Hod the poisoned spear and then directed him where to throw it. The spear went right through Baldur and killed him.

Norse tales mention a place called Gnipa Cave that likely refers to the Underworld. Like an open grave, it's entrance led to the realm of the dead

After Baldur's death, Hermod was sent as a messenger to bring him back from the Underworld. But Hel would not give up her prize easily. She made a deal to only release Baldur if everything in the worlds wept for him.

Hermod and the gods agreed. They sent messengers throughout the universe to bring news of Baldur's fate. Everything did weep for Baldur, except for one.

Loki, ever the trickster, had disguised himself as a giantess. When he was asked if he wept for Baldur, he refused.

So the deal between the gods and Hel was off. She kept Baldur in her great hall, showing that she had power and authority over the dead in the Underworld—even over the gods.

The Figures of NORSE MYTHOLOGY

Angrboda: (AHN-guhr-boh-dah) a giantess and the mother of Loki's children

Baldur: a beautiful and well-loved god, son of Odin and Frigg

Fenrir: a giant wolf, the son of Loki and Angrboda, and Hel's sibling

Frigg: a goddess, Odin's wife and mother to Baldur

Garm: a huge hound who guarded the entrance to the Underworld

Hel: the daughter of Loki and Angrboda and ruler of the Underworld

Hermod: the messenger god and a son of Odin

Hod: the blind god and a son of Odin

Loki: the trickster god, son of Farbauti and Laufey

Jormungand: (YOR-moon-gahnd) a giant snake that circled the world, also known as the Midgard serpent. He was the son of Loki and Angrboda, and Hel's sibling.

Modgud: (MOD-good) a giantess and fierce fighter who guarded the Gjöll Bridge in the Underworld.

Nidhogg: (NEED-hog) a serpent or dragon who sucked the blood from the dead and gnawed on the roots of the World Tree, Yggdrasil (IG-drah-sihl).

Odin: the ruler of the gods, the creator of the cosmos, and the All-father

Thor: the god of thunder and a son of Odin

Tyr: (TEER) the god of war and a son of Odin

Other Paths to Explore

>>> When Baldur had nightmares about his own death, Odin used his magic to summon a wise woman from her grave. When he asked who would kill Baldur, she answered, "Hod." Odin now knew that Baldur's dreams would come true. Imagine that Odin had not spoken with the old woman. How would the story be different if the gods never knew that Baldur's dreams would come true?

>>> After Frigg made everything in the Universe promise not to harm Baldur, she thought her son would be safe. But later, a spear poisoned with mistletoe killed Baldur. What does this mean about the gods' fates? Can they be changed?

>>> Loki was the Norse god of trickery. He also greatly disliked Odin's son, Baldur. Why do you think Loki was so jealous of Baldur? What could the gods have done differently to avoid the tragedy of Baldur's death? What would have happened if Loki had not played his tricks on the gods?

Bibliography

Anderson, Rasmus B., trans. *The Younger Edda*. Reprint of the 1901 Chicago edition, Project Gutenberg, 2006. https://www.gutenberg.org/files/18947/18947-h/18947-h.htm

Ashliman, D. L. "The Norse Creation Myth." Folklore and Mythology Electronic Texts. University of Pittsburgh, February 17, 2010. https://sites.pitt.edu/~dash/creation.html.

Bellows, Henry Adams, trans. *The Poetic Edda*. Reprint of the 1936 Princeton edition, Internet Sacred Text Archive. John Bruno Hare, 2001. https://www.sacred-texts.com/neu/poe/index.htm.

Brodeur, Arthur Gilchrist, trans. *The Prose Edda*. New York: American-Scandinavian Foundation, 1916.

Byock, Jesse L., trans. *The Saga of the Volsungs: The Norse Epic of Sigurd the Dragon Slayer*. Berkeley: University of California Press, 1990.

Gaiman, Neil. *Norse Mythology*. 1st ed. New York: W. W. Norton & Company, 2017.

Hopkins, Joseph, J. H. Roberts, Ross Downing, Lauren E. Fountain, and Arjuna Thomassen. "Mimisbrunnr.info: Developments in Ancient Germanic Studies." Mimisbrunnr.info: Developments in Ancient Germanic Studies, December 1, 2021. https://www.mimisbrunnr.info/.

McCoy, Daniel. "The Ultimate Online Guide to Norse Mythology and Religion." Norse Mythology for Smart People, February 8, 2019. https://norse-mythology.org/.

Sturluson, Snorri. *Edda*. Translated by Anthony Faulkes. Viking Society for Northern Research. London: J. M. Dent, 2002. http://vsnrweb-publications.org.uk/.

Glossary

battalion (buh-TAL-yuhn)—a military unit that may include hundreds or thousands of soldiers who work and fight in combat together

desperate (DEH-spuh-ruht)—feeling an urgent need for something when there is little hope of getting it

fate (FAYT)—the things that will happen in the future; a controlling power

invincible (in-VIN-suh-buhl)—impossible to defeat; unbeatable

mead (MEED)—a wine-like drink made from water, honey, and yeast

oath (OHTH)—a serious, formal promise

ransom (RAN-suhm)—money or objects that are demanded to be paid in order to free someone who is being held captive

turbulent (TUR-byuh-luhnt)—moving quickly and violently

venomous (VEH-nuh-muhs)—able to produce and deliver a poison, usually by biting or stinging

Read More

Loh-Hagan, Virginia. *Hel*. Ann Arbor, MI: Cherry Lake Publishing, 2019.

Bowen, Carl, Michael Dahl, and Louise Simonson. *Gods and Thunder: A Graphic Novel of Old Norse Myths*. North Mankato, MN: Capstone Young Readers, 2017.

Ralphs, Matt. *Norse Myths*. New York: DK Publishing, 2021.

Internet Sites

Hel: Goddess
norse-mythology.org/gods-and-creatures/giants/hel/

Hel: Realm
mythopedia.com/topics/hel-realm

Helheim: The Underworld
blog.vkngjewelry.com/en/helheim-the-underworld/

Norse Mythology Facts for Kids
kids.kiddle.co/Norse_mythology#Cosmology

About the Author

Photo by Karon Dubke, Capstone.

Gina Kammer never grew out of Narnia and Middle-earth. Instead, she went on to study their medieval source texts, mythology, theater, and other literature at Bethany Lutheran College, Richmond University in London, and finally the University of South Dakota for her M.A. degree. Now she's an author, editor, and book coach specializing in science fiction and fantasy. She also occasionally teaches writing courses. Her other interests include tea, traveling, oil painting, archery, and snuggling her grumpy bunny. She lives among piles of books in Minnesota with her husband, daughter, and menagerie of critters. Find her at ginakammer.com.